HANAE MORI
STYLE

HANAE MORI STYLE

KODANSHA INTERNATIONAL
Tokyo · New York · London

Supervised by Hanae Mori
Edited by Yasuko Suita
Designed by Ikko Tanaka

"Beyond the Century" on pages 18 to 31:
Photographs by Kishin Shinoyama
Hair by Seiichi Okuhara (Shiseido Beauty Creation Center)
Makeup by Noriko Okubo (Shiseido Beauty Creation Center)

"East Meets West" Hanae Mori Exhibition at Art Tower Mito on pages 33 to 110:
Photographs by Hiroshi Yoda
Installation by Larry Laslo

Distributed in the United States by Kodansha America, Inc., 575 Lexington Avenue, New York, NY 10022, and in the United Kingdom and continental Europe by Kodansha Europe Ltd., 95 Aldwych, London WC2B 4JF. Published by Kodansha International Ltd., 17-14 Otowa 1-chome, Bunkyo-ku, Tokyo 112-8652, and Kodansha America, Inc.
Copyright © 2001 by HANAE MORI Co., Ltd., and Kodansha International Ltd.
All rights reserved. Printed in Japan.
First edition, 2001

01 02 03 04   10 9 8 7 6 5 4 3 2 1
ISBN 4-7700-2684-6

www.thejapanpage.com

Photograph by Richard Avedon

Hanae Mori: The Symphonist

Hidekazu Yoshida

Hanae Mori's fondness for butterflies is well known. At a showing of her work held at a museum in Japan, one whole room was devoted to works employing the butterfly motif.

Her preoccupation with butterflies is more than just a hobby: I remember someone once likening the essence of Mori's creativity to a butterfly whose two wings symbolize both the separateness of East and West and their need to come together in a pair if they are to achieve completeness. The same attractive metaphor, in fact, applies not just to Ms. Mori herself, but to all the work done by artists in post-Meiji Restoration Japan, where the newly introduced Western art posed ineluctable questions for artistic creation.

In Mori's own case, her guiding principle, it would seem, has been to master basic Western-style structures, then to embellish them with designs embodying Oriental—in practice, mainly Japanese—colors and forms. The approach is similar (in a field more familiar to a music critic like myself) to that of post-Meiji Japanese composers. Seen in this light, most of Mori's creations correspond, not to the type of experimental, avant-garde composition prized by a connoisseur minority, but to larger-scale, more conventional symphonic music. The clothes she produces have a star-quality brilliance that appeals to most people at first glance, together with, at a deeper level, a more positive, dynamic impact. At the same time, there is enough of the spirit of experiment, of readiness to tackle the new, backed up by a sureness of technique in translating it into form, to win the approval both of the truly sophisticated viewer (in musical terms, the experienced listener) and of the actual specialist. In this respect, she could be called, in musical terms, a "symphonist."

Probably it is this combination of the two sides that makes it possible for her to work, to create, not only in haute couture but in the more practical field of prêt-à-porter as well. This latter ability, I feel, does not signify a conscious aiming at the popular market so much as the natural bent toward the nonexclusive seen in her abundant ideas for clothing for active wear. The fact that Beethoven, say, or Mahler attracts large numbers of listeners does not make either of them a "mass" composer in the vulgar sense.

I first became acquainted with Mori the artist in her capacity as a designer of costumes for opera. The first occasion was the La Scala *Madama Butterfly* produced by Keita Asari. The next was *Elektra* at the 1997 Salzburg Festival, also produced by Asari, for which she designed the costumes. The latter in particular were magnificent. Asari's production was itself unusual, rejecting the traditional German expressionist approach, with its stage shrouded in gloomy darkness and its bright red fires or crimson blood leaping and splashing at every twist in the plot, in favor of a view of the drama as a tragedy of close-kinship hatred enacted amidst the relentless heat and glare of an island floating in the intense blue of the Mediterranean and lit by an all-pervasive sunshine. The characters moved, suffered, and died within an ancient landscape, amidst a fierce interplay of light and color.

The three principal characters are all women—a mother, the daughter, and the latter's younger sister, to whom Ms. Mori allotted purple, black, and blue costumes respectively. After a scene in which the blue and black figures join in bewailing their lot and arguing with each other, their mother, the queen Clytemnestra, makes her first appearance. At this point, Ms. Mori devised a scene in which a figure, fluttering a seemingly endless veil of deep lilac, appeared without warning as though bursting through the draperies covering her from head to foot. It was a breathtaking, spellbinding moment. Luxury and sensuality, dignity and pride were all combined in that one figure. At that moment, I realized for the first time something essential about Mori's work.

To explain that work as Western structure plus Japanese decoration is not, in itself, adequate. The point is that she backs the latter up with "action." Her colors are colors that "dance," her forms are forms that pulse with life.

Generally speaking, Japanese artists, in the fine arts as elsewhere, make their profoundest statements via stillness and silence. The messages of the tea ceremony and of, say, a majority of Toru Takemitsu's compositions are equally concerned with the weight of silence, the value of motion arrested. So it is with Mori's work; but here again her originality interposes a characteristic dynamism. This can be seen, for example, in the not inconsiderable influence exerted on her clothes by the designs encircling the skirt of the traditional kimono above the hem.

There is decoration, of course, at the bottom of garments in the West too: one thinks of the huge skirt worn by the Infanta in Velásquez' *Las Meninas,* or the heavy decoration around the bottom of the tubular skirts fashionable in the France of Napoleon III. In these, however, shifting balances in the clothing as a whole, which create variety in the visual composition, are the determining factor, whereas the pattern of the Japanese kimono leaves the form of it, as such, untouched.

The kimono creates a special beauty when the wearer is sitting quietly in formal Japanese style, with the legs folded beneath the body; when she moves, it is done so as to shift the center of gravity, to change the position, as gently and inconspicuously as possible. Essentially, moreover, the kimono aims to avoid decoration on the upper half of the body and to create a clean, simple form. Thus the effect is all the more brilliant and striking when the wearer finally stands up, revealing the pattern extending around the bottom of the skirt.

Hanae Mori is perfectly aware of this process; she does not reject stillness, but at certain moments she will create an effect of beauty by deliberately upsetting it. It is in such moments that I see the butterfly—the butterfly that, resting till now with its two wings folded together like the sails of a ship, suddenly and silently rises into the air in a movement that combines lightness and elegance with a powerful underlying life-force.

Director General, Art Tower Mito   Music Critic

シンフォニーの作曲家・森 英恵

吉田秀和

森英恵さんは蝶が好きだという。水戸芸術館で展示会を開催した時も、一室を彼女の蝶のコレクションにあてたが見事なものだった。

彼女の蝶好みは單なるホビーではなく、蝶はその二枚の翼で西洋と東洋という別々のものであって、しかも一対となった時初めて完全になるものの象徴でもあり、これこそ彼女の制作の本質に通じるものだという話をきいた覚えもある。しかし、この美しい喩えは森さんだけでなく、近代日本の芸術家の仕事の全体に通じるものがあり、西洋の芸術の提出したものにどう対決するかは、近代日本の芸術創造にとって避けて通れない課題だった。

その中で、森さんのお仕事は、西洋の骨組を自分の身につけながら、そこに東洋——といっても日本が主だが——の色と形を意匠化して服飾とするという道筋をとるものだったように見える。これは私の身近かの明治以来の音楽家たちの仕事にもみられることで、その中で森さんの制作は、少数の通人に珍重される実験的尖端芸術を志向するというのでなくて、スケールの大きな交響音楽を描くようなものだというように、私には思われる。彼女の衣裳は多くの人が一目見た途端にパッと引きつけられるようなスター的華やかさと、人々の心をゆすぶるような行動的積極的働きかけをもった作品になっている。それでいて、また、本当に目の肥えた人（音楽でいえば、耳の良いきき手）、あるいは専門家にもなるほどと思わせる新しいものに挑戦してゆく実験精神と、それを形に仕立てる技術の確かさの裏づけがある。そういう点で、彼女は音楽でいえば、シンフォニー作曲家と呼ぶことのできるタイプと思われる。この両面があるので、森さんはオート・クチュールだけでなく、プレタ・ポルテの実用芸術の畑でも仕事ができる人なのだろう。それは大衆向けを狙うというより、自然と大衆性に通じてゆく、たとえば行動性に富む服装のアイディアにも富んだ素質ということになるのではなかろうか。ベートーヴェンやマーラーは大勢のきき手をひきつけるからといって大衆の人とはいえないのである。

美術家としての森さんを、私が、初めて知ったのはオペラの衣裳担当者としてだった。最初はミラノのスカラ座で浅利慶太さんが演出した『蝶々夫人』の時だが、そのあと一九九七年のザルツブルグのフェスティヴァルでの『エレクトラ』で彼女が受けもった衣裳。これが素晴らしかった。浅利さんの演出も変っていて、彼はこの劇が普通ドイツ表現派の伝統によって、

全体として暗く陰鬱な舞台の中で、筋の節々に真紅の烽火の炎が燃え上がったり、真赤な血があたり一面にとびちるといった形になるのに背を向け、底の抜けるほど真青な地中海にとりまかれ、そこに浮ぶ孤島のさんさんたる陽に照らされ、ぎらぎらした熱と光の中で起る肉親相喰む悲劇として構想した。劇中の人物は、強烈な光と色の交代する古代風風景の中で動きまわり、苦しみ、死ぬ。

主な登場人物は母と娘とその妹の三人の女たち。森さんはその三人に紫、黒、青の衣裳を配分した。そうして黒と青が相寄り嘆いたり争ったりするあと、母の王妃が登場する段になって、森さんはそれを、濃いリラ紫の長い長いヴェールの被衣の裳裾をひるがえして、何かをつきやぶるようにして突如として一人の形姿が立ち現われる場としてつくった。それは満場の客がみんな言葉を失い、思わず息をのむ瞬間、まさに呪縛の瞬間だった。豪奢と淫美、気品とおごりが一体となった姿。それをみて、私は森さんの何者であるかを認識したのだった。森さんの仕事を西洋の構造に日本の装飾を加えたものというだけでは何を言ったことにもならない。森さんはそこに「行動性」という裏づけを与えた。彼女のは「踊る色彩」「躍動する形象」というべきものなのだ。一般に日本の美術家芸術家は静止と寡黙の中で深いものを表わそうとする。茶の湯にしろ、武満徹の多くの作品にしろ、その底には沈黙の重み、休止の尊さがある。森さんにもそれがある。けれども彼女の独創はそこにも「動き」を入れる。たとえば、彼女の衣裳ではキモノの裾模様が果たす役割も小さくない。西洋にだって服の下部に飾りがないわけではない。ベラスケスの王女の肖像の巨大なスカート、ナポレオン三世時代の筒形のスカート……すべては服装全体のバランスの移動とかかわり、構造的変化をひきおこす。日本の裾模様は着物の形には手をつけない。

着物は静かに正座した姿が美しいが、動く時はできるだけゆるやかで目立たぬよう重心を移し位置を変える。それに着物でも、もともと上半身は飾りを避け清楚な姿を心がけている。それだけに立ち上がると、着物の下半身に大きくおかれた裾模様はひときわ鮮やかに人目をひく。森さんはこれを見逃さなかった。静止の美を廃しはしないが、ある瞬間突如として破調の美を出現さす。私はそこに舟の帆のように二枚の羽根を重ねて憩っていた蝶が音もなく突然飛び立った時の軽快と優雅と活発な生命力の一体化をみる。　水戸芸術館館長 音楽評論家

Hanae Mori: The Iron Butterfly

Suzy Menkes

"Fusion fashion" is now as stylish as "fusion food." The flavors of lemon grass and sushi on Western tables have permeated fashion as a passion for all things Oriental.

Designers view flat-plane kimono geometry and Pacific Rim pajamas with an enthusiasm not seen since Japonisme was in vogue a century ago. In the age of cyber design and computer-enhanced prints, the gentle brushstrokes and stylized Japanese flowers that captivated Van Gogh and his fellow artists are a current source of inspiration.

In this history of East–West fashion, no one has bridged the cultural divide with more skill and subtlety than Hanae Mori. Her work continues to express an ongoing dialogue between Japanese tradition and French couture, within the context of modern women's lives.

Both in her forty-year oeuvre and in her personal odyssey as a creative businesswoman, Madame Mori has been a pioneer. With her husband Ken Mori's unstinting support, she became the first female Japanese fashion entrepreneur in a man's world. Yet she retained a sense of family that has born fruit in the next generation.

She translated the bravura and dash of theater costume into the swoosh of an evening gown, and the practical demands of actors on stage or screen into sleek tailoring.

In the artistry and complexity of her spirit, Madame Mori remains Japanese, despite the modernity of her outlook and her own streamlined, globe-trotting uniform. She has successfully united the European sensibility of personal expression with a deep belief in the importance of learning the form, the Kata, the proper way of doing things.

Often, like onion-skin layers of kimonos, Madame Mori hides one skill behind another. First to meet the eye is the fabric and its decoration: delicate prints, bringing color and pattern; tactile textures from raw silk through deep-pile cashmere; and embellishment of appliquéd roses or those signature butterflies.

Then there is needlecraft, when tiny pleats shape a bodice or fan across a skirt. Rivulets of ruffles, graceful drapes and a lattice of ribbons are all couture effects done with effortless ease.

Underpinning this lightness of hand and attitude is incisive cutting that can make an ethereal bias-cut chiffon gown or a tailored suit flow to the contours of the body. The result is an absolute mastery of the Western skill of cutting and sewing that is still perfumed with Japanese spirit.

For this steely framework to her imaginative work and for her own courage and determination, Madame Mori deserves to be given a new title: the Iron Butterfly.

Fashion Editor, *International Herald Tribune*

ハナエ・モリ——鉄の蝶

スージー・メンカス

いま食の世界では無国籍料理がもてはやされているが、ファッションの世界でも"融合"が今様である。レモングラスや寿司の風味が西欧の食卓に登場するごとく、オリエンタルなものならなんでもという風潮が、ファッションの世界にも浸透してきた。

デザイナー達は、平面裁ちの着物の幾何学や東南アジアのゆったりしたパンツに、一世紀昔、ジャポニズムが流行して以来の熱狂ぶりである。サイバーデザインとコンピュータープリントの時代に、ゴッホやその仲間のアーティスト達を虜にしたやわらかな水墨の筆づかいや日本の花の図案が、発想源となっているのだ。

東と西のファッションの歴史の中で、森英恵ほど巧妙かつ精微に異文化の狭間に橋をかけた人は他にいない。現代女性の暮らしという場をかりて、日本の伝統とフランスのクチュールの絶え間ない対話という形で、仕事を続けている。

40年に及ぶ制作活動、そして創造的な女性事業家としての冒険、そのいずれにおいてもマダム森はパイオニアであった。夫君、森賢の惜しみない支援を受けて、男性社会であったファッション界で最初の日本人女性事業家となったのだ。それでいて、彼女は家庭感覚を大切にすることを忘れなかったのだが、そのことは次の世代に立派に実を結んでいるといえよう。

舞台衣裳の華麗さ、見栄えをイブニングドレスの衣擦れに、舞台や銀幕の役者達が求める機能性をしっかりとした仕立てに、昇華させた。

現代的な視野をもち、自らつくる合理的な衣服に身を包んで世界をかけ廻っているが、その精神の芸術性、複雑さにおいて、彼女はまぎれもない日本人である。まさに彼女は、個性の表現を重んじる西欧の感性と日本固有の型をうまく使いこなす深い洞察力とを、見事に一体化することに成功した。

玉ねぎの皮のように幾重にも層をなす着物同様、マダム森は一つの技の裏にもう一つ別の技を隠しもっている。まず眼に入るのは布地、その美しさ、繊細な染め、色と柄、未晒しの絹から毛あしの長いカシミアまで手ざわりのいい織物。そして、バラのアップリケやその署名ともいうべき蝶。そして、仕立て。こまかなプリーツが身体の線をなぞり、扇のようにスカートに広がる。流れるようなラッフル、優美なドレープ、リボンの網代編み、これらクチュールの技をいともらくらくと駆使している。

この手際のよさと心意気を支えるのは鋭い裁断だ。それは、空気のように軽やかなバイヤス裁ちのシフォンのドレスや身体の線にそって流れるテーラードスーツを可能にする。これらは、裁断と縫製という西洋の技術を、完璧にものにしての成果だが、そこにはやはりいまも日本の心が馥郁と香っている。その想像力に富んだ仕事をしっかりと位置づけるために、また彼女自身の勇気と決意を称えるために、マダム森は新しい称号が与えられよう……それは"鉄の蝶"。

『インターナショナル・ヘラルド・トリビューン』ファッション・エディター

Beyond the Century
Photographs by Kishin Shinoyama

East Meets West
Hanae Mori Exhibition
at Art Tower Mito

Photographs by Hiroshi Yoda / Installation by Larry Laslo

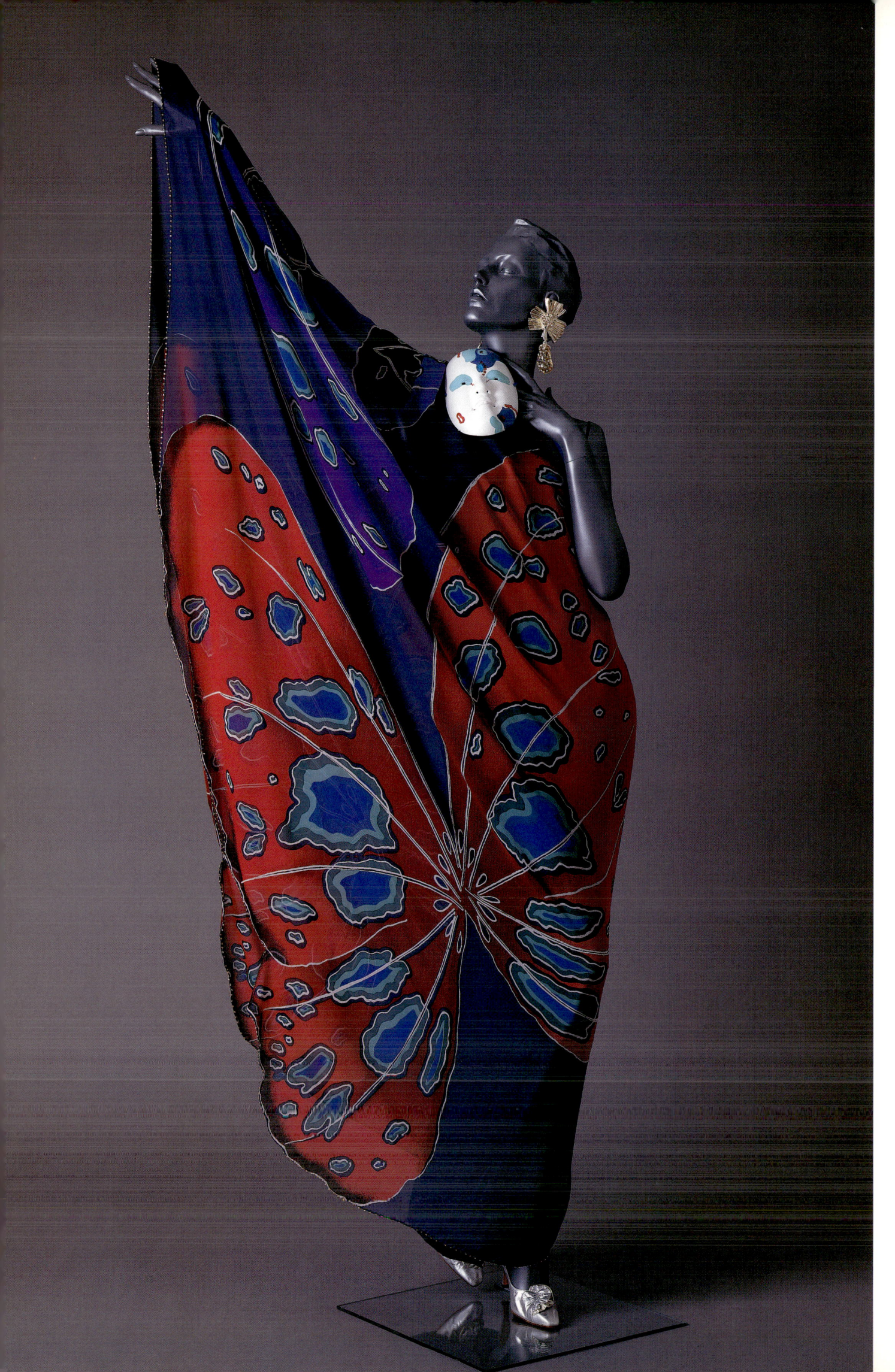

List of Works

S/S Spring/Summer
F/W Fall/Winter

18–19 Black lace spangle-embroidered evening dress   2000 F/W
       Rainbow silk and tulle layering flower petal dress   '96 S/S
20–21 Butterflies of bronze and black flutter   '95 F/W
22–23 Art Deco mousseline tunic (violet)   2000 F/W
       Art Deco mousseline tunic (blue)   2000 F/W
24   Jumpsuit in gold point lace   2000 F/W
25   Black alligator jacket over snakeskin print tulle skirt   2000 F/W
26–27 Asymmetrical sheath dress in kimono fabric   2000 F/W
       Turquoise silk crepe dress embroidered with flowers   2000 F/W
28–29 Black lace evening ensemble   '97 F/W
       Black evening dress   '98 F/W
30–31 Wedding dress in tulle   2000 F/W

33   Salvia red short dress   '95 S/S
34   White daisy dress   '88 S/S
35   Woman in calla lily   '88 S/S
36   Platinum velvet evening dress   '84 F/W
37   Black lace and rose organza evening dress   '99 S/S
38   Rose dress   '92 S/S
39, 42–43 Silk satin dress with rose   '90 F/W
40–41 White flower dress   '81 S/S
       Bustier dress with large flower   '81 S/S
44   Silk georgette evening dress with white flowers   '80 S/S
45   Magenta pink flower dress in silk faille   '91 S/S
46   Silk crepe evening dress with embroidered peonies   '98 S/S
47   Cherry blossom beaded dress   '85 S/S
48   Dress with beaded trim jacket   '90 S/S
49   Woman in tulip   '88 S/S
50   New-grass green dress with small flowers   '95 S/S

53   Pink suede suit with gold butterflies   '87 S/S
54   Black silk dress embroidered with ribbon belt   '83 S/S
55   Silk georgette evening dress with embroidered butterflies   '92 F/W
56   Silk butterfly dress with gold and silver beading   '86 F/W
57   Art Nouveau butterfly dress   '90 S/S
58   Butterfly dress   '81 S/S
59   Red butterfly dress   '90 S/S
60   Patchwork jacket and draped skirt   '94 S/S
61   Black kimono coat / Cubist dress in embroidered mousseline   '99 S/S

62–63	Abstract print evening dress with stole '97 F/W	100	Sailor suit in navy, red, and white '82 S/S
64	Beige chiffon evening dress with apple blossoms '98 S/S	101	Silk crepe sailor dress with embroidered tie '83 S/S

62–63   Abstract print evening dress with stole   '97 F/W
64   Beige chiffon evening dress with apple blossoms   '98 S/S

66   Sequined evening dress   '97 F/W
67   Black draped cape and sheath dress   '88 F/W
68–69   Black evening dress with ostrich feather   '96 F/W
70   *Lion King*—panther chiffon short evening dress   '98 S/S
   Lion King—zebra print evening dress   '98 S/S
71   Ensemble with zebra jacket and feather collar   '95 F/W
   Short evening ensemble embroidered with a panther   '92 F/W
72   White hooded short coat trimmed with mink / Satin waistcoat and pants   '99 F/W
73   Mink trimmed cashmere shift dress with cape   '89 F/W
74   Feather ball gown in taffeta   '88 F/W
75   Tweed long dress with silver fox stole   '98 F/W
76   Burgundy and gold chiffon dress   '98 F/W
77   Royal blue silk crepe dress   '98 F/W
78   Leopard beaded ensemble   '81 S/S
   Leopard dress in gold   '81 S/S

80   Pearl dress   '85 S/S
81   Beaded chiffon dress depicting Japanese autumn   '98 F/W
82   Dragon dress in chiffon and satin   '93 F/W
83   Kabuki evening dress   '93 F/W
84–85   Dragon evening ensemble   '93 F/W
86   Black and white Sumie dress in chiffon   '89 S/S
87   Black and white Sumie chiffon dress with stole   '89 S/S
88   Wisteria silk crepe dress   '98 S/S
89   Hokusai-inspired mist and mountains on a dress   '96 S/S
90   Obi evening coat   '68 F/W

92–93   Hand-painted butterflies over a fully skirted dress of green tea   '96 F/W
   Butterfly dress embroidered by Lesage   '92 F/W
94   Monotone suit—navy blue and white wool   '92 S/S
95   Suit in white and marine blue   '83 S/S
96   Navy blue suit in wool crepe   '87 S/S
97   Waves and clouds—white and blue suit   '91 S/S
98   Metallic gray crepe evening dress   '97 S/S
99   Silver evening dress   '93 S/S

100   Sailor suit in navy, red, and white   '82 S/S
101   Silk crepe sailor dress with embroidered tie   '83 S/S
102   Bustier dress and bolero in the colors of the sun   '94 F/W
103   Russian cashmere coat with astrakhan   '87 F/W
104   Fuschia chiffon evening dress decorated with feathers (pink)   '97 S/S
105   Monaco blue fine draped satin dress with stole   '89 F/W
106   Stripes of ebony and single roses adorning a double skirted dress   '96 S/S
107   Black evening dress with painted silver roses   '97 F/W

109   Multicolored cellophane lace cocktail dress embroidered with feathers   '99 F/W
110   Feather and embroidery jacket   '92 F/W

Brief Personal History

At the salon in Shinjuku (1950's)

Fitting for Nobuko Otowa (1950's)

With Alberto Giacometti in Paris (1961)

1926	Born in Shimane Prefecture, Japan.
1947	Graduates from Tokyo Woman's Christian University, Japanese Literature Dept. Marries Ken Mori, goes to dressmaking school.
1951	Opens first atelier in Shinjuku.
1954	Starts designing costumes for the cinema. Over the next seven years works as a designer for over three hundred films, including *Crazed Fruit* (1956) by Ko Nakahira; *Forty-Eight-Year-Old Rebel* (1956) by Kozaburo Yoshimura; *Early Autumn* (1958) by Yasujiro Ozu; *A Cruel Story of Youth* (1960) by Nagisa Oshima.
1965	Is invited by the American fashion world, and presents her first collection overseas in New York, which is acclaimed as "East Meets West."
1966	Travels to India at the invitation of the Tourist Bureau of the Indian Government.
1967	Designs uniforms for the flight attendants of Japan Air Lines, likewise in 1970, in celebration of the first jumbo jet, and again in 1977. Contract for bed linen with West Point Pepperell Co. in New York.
1969	Hanae Mori Fragrance is launched in U.S.A. by Shiseido Co., Ltd. Contract with Joseph Bancroft & Sons Co.—presents Ban-Lon Collection in New York and Tokyo. Contract with the Handicrafts and Handlooms Export Corporation of India and presents Hanae Mori Made in India collection. "East Meets West"—participates in the Fortnight Celebration at Neiman Marcus in Dallas. The film "The World of Hanae Mori" is produced.
1970	Designs uniforms for the hostesses of the Steel Pavilion and Fuji Group Pavilion at EXPO '70 held in Osaka. Hanae Mori Boutique at the Waldorf Astoria Hotel is inaugurated.
1973	Launches Bed & Bath clothes by Nishikawa Sangyo Co., Ltd. Opens House of Hanae Mori in New York on East 79th St. Next year opens a showroom for ready-to-wear line at 550 Seventh Avenue.
1974	Participates in the Japan Fortnight at Neiman Marcus and presents her collection.
1975	Is invited to Monaco by H.S.H. Princess Grace for the opening of the Hotel Loews. Shows her collection there and later in Paris for the first time. Designs costumes for the play *A Ghost Is Here* by Kobo Abe.
1976	Holds fashion show, The World of Hanae Mori, at the Seibu Theater in Tokyo.

With Oleg Cassini in New York (1961)

At the Japanese Embassy, London (1972)

Opening of the showroom in New York (1973)

With Stanley Marcus in Dallas (1974)

	Designs the costumes for the ballet *The Fisherman and His Soul* at the request of H.S.H. Princess Grace of Monaco.
1977	Inaugurates her Haute Couture Maison at 17–19 Avenue Montaigne in Paris and presents her Haute Couture Collection.
	Becomes a member of La Chambre Syndicale de la Couture Parisienne.
1978	Inaugurates the HANAE MORI Building on Omotesando, Tokyo, designed by Kenzo Tange.
	Is invited to China to lecture on design.
1979	Contract with Franklin Mint Co., Ltd., for direct marketing business.
1981	Organizes French Film Festival in cooperation with National Unifrance Film to show new French films in Japan.
1985	Designs the costumes for *Madama Butterfly* at La Scala in Milan.
1986	Designs costumes for the Paris Opera ballet *Cinderella* directed by Rudolf Nureyev.
	Participates in the exhibition Avant-Garde Japon 1910–1970 at the Centre Pompidou in Paris.
1987	Designs costumes of the musical *Evita* for Shiki Theatrical Company, followed by *The Naked King* (1988), *Ondine* (1988), *A Dream Awoken from a Dream* (1988), *The Cat Who Wished to Be a Man* (1989), *Ri Koran* (1991).
	Launches school uniform for Akashi Hifuku Kogyo Co., Ltd.
1988	Designs the Seoul Olympics swimming costume for Miss Mikako Kotani, a bronze medalist.
1989	Designs costumes for the French film *L'Amante*.
	Holds Hanae Mori Exhibition to commemorate her 35th anniversary as a fashion designer, with international tour: Pavillon des Arts in Paris (1990), Musée Océanographique in Monaco (1990).
	Awarded Chevalier dans l'Ordre National de la Légion d'Honneur by French Government.
1990	Presents Hanae Mori Rose created by Georges Delbard in Paris.
1992	Designs the official uniforms for the Japanese Delegation at Barcelona 25th Olympic Games.
	Holds Hanae Mori and Paris Haute Couture Exhibition at the Kobe City Museum as main event of the 4th Kobe Fashion Festival.
	Opens Hanae Mori Boutique at Place de l'Alma in Paris.
1993	Designs the Executive Floors for the opening of the Rihga Royal Hotel in Kokura.
	Creates the bridal gown, robe décolletée, for Crown Princess Masako for the imperial wedding.
1994	Designs the official uniforms for Japanese delegation to the 17th

Invited to Monaco by H.S.H. Princess Grace (center) (1975)

At the White House with President Reagan and Prime Minister Suzuki (1981)

At "The Best Five '83" in Tokyo with Valentino Garavani and Sonia Rykiel (1982)

Madama Butterfly at La Scala (1985)

Olympic Winter Games in Lillehammer.

Participates in the exhibition Japonism in Fashion at Kyoto Costume Institute. International tour: Musée de la Mode et du Costume in Paris (1996), TFT Hall in Tokyo (1996), Los Angeles County Museum (1998).

Produces a recital by Izumi Yukimura and designs her costumes to commemorate her 40th anniversary as a singer.

Participates in the exhibition Japanese Design: A Survey since 1950 at the Philadelphia Museum of Art. International tour: Galleria del Triennale in Milan (1995), Stadtische Kunsthalle in Dusseldorf (1995), Centre Pompidou in Paris (1995–1996), Suntory Museum in Osaka (1996).

Participates in the exhibition Orientalism—Visions of the East in Western Dress at the Metropolitan Museum of Art in New York.

1995 Participates in the exhibition Bloom at the Metropolitan Museum of Art in New York.

Presents Parfum Hanae Mori in Paris.

Participates in the exhibition Haute Couture at the Metropolitan Museum of Art in New York.

1996 Designs costumes for the opera *Elektra* for the 1996 Salzburg Festival in Austria.

Awarded the Order of Culture by the Emperor of Japan.

1997 Designs costumes for the Noh play *Takayama Ukon*. Performances: Tokyo (1997 and 1999), Kanazawa (1998), Kusatsu (1999), Paris (1999), Nagoya (2000).

1998 Holds Hanae Mori Exhibition ("Hanae Mori and Paris—20 Years of Paris Haute Couture") in Tokyo for the Year of France in Japan. Tour: Kasama Nichido Museum of Art in Ibaraki (1998).

Is appointed President of Mito Arts Foundation.

2000 Designs costumes for the repeat performance of the Paris Opera ballet *Cinderella*.

Holds exhibition Seeing, Wearing, Transcending—Two Centuries Moved by Fashion ("Hanae Mori Exhibition: Meeting of the East and West" and "Millennium Collections: Tokyo, Paris, Asia, New York, and Japan") at Art Tower Mito as a special event to commemorate ATM's 10th anniversary.

Moves her Haute Couture Maison to 5 Place de l'Alma in Paris.

2001 Designs tapestries for the Muikaichi Spa—Yu Ra Ra in her hometown in Shimane.

Designs The World of Orchid "Butterfly Flies" as part of the Japan Grand Prix—International Orchid Festival 2001.

Awarded the order of culture by the Emperor (1996)

Chevalier dans l'Ordre National de la Légion d'Honneur (1989)

Hanae Mori Exhibition in Paris with Mme. Chirac (1990)

With models in Beijing (1997)

Awards

The 4th Japan Fashion Editors' Club Award for creating film costumes (1960)

The Rex Award from Maison Blanche in New Orleans (1967, 1970, 1976)

The Neiman Marcus Award (1973)

Le Diplôme de L'Excellence Européenne in France (1978)

The 7th Pioneer Award of Tama Morita in Japan (1978)

The Symbol of Man Award from the Minnesota Museum (1978)

La Médaille d'Argent de la Ville de Paris in France (1978)

The Best Award from the National Chamber of Italian High Fashion in Rome (1978)

Woman of Quality Award from the Diamond Information Center of the United States (1983)

La Croix de Chevalier des Arts et des Lettres by the French Ministry of Culture in Paris (1984)

Night of Stars Award from the Fashion Group in U.S.A. (1987)

The Asahi Prize as a pioneer of Japanese fashion from the *Asahi Shimbun* (1988)

Purple Ribbon Decoration from Emperor Showa (1988)

Blasons Otard 1989 from La Maison de Cognac Otard in France (1989)

Chevalier dans l'Ordre National de la Légion d'Honneur by French Government (1989)

Person of Cultural Merit by Japanese Government (1989)

The 5th Louise Pommery Award from Pommery S.A. and Mercian Corporation in Japan (1993)

The 13th Women's Warrior Award from Asia Pacific Women's Network in Los Angeles (1994)

The 11th Tokyo Metropolitan Cultural Award from Tokyo Metropolitan Government (1995)

Distinguished Achievement Award from the Japanese Women's Society of Honolulu (1995)

Awarded by the Asian-American Federation of New York as "a distinguished individual whose pursuit of excellence has left an indelible mark on fashion design" (1995)

Creativity '95 Award for an advertisement for '95 S/S Hanae Mori Haute Couture (photo by Richard Avedon) from the Art Directors Club and *Art Direction* Magazine in U.S.A. (1995)

The Order of Culture from the Emperor of Japan (1996)

The 8th Japan Jewelry Best-Dresser Award (1997)

The 40th Japan Fashion Editors' Club Special Award (1997)

Deborah Award from the Anti-Defamation League in Los Angeles (1997)

Chevalier du Tastevin from La Confrérie des Chevaliers du Tastevin in France (1998)

Books

Designing for Tomorrow (1979)

A Glass Butterfly (1984)

HANAE MORI 1960–1989 (1989)

Fashion—A Butterfly That Flew Across the Border (1993)

With young Thai designers at Art Tower Mito (2000)

Hanae Mori Exhibition "East Meets West" (2000)

HANAE MORI STYLE

2001年7月13日　第1刷発行

監修 ──────── 森　英恵
編集 ──────── 吹田靖子
写真 ──────── 篠山紀信／与田弘志
デザイン ────── 田中一光

発行者 ─────── 野間佐和子
発行所 ─────── 講談社インターナショナル株式会社
　　　　　　　　〒112-8652　東京都文京区音羽1-17-14
　　　　　　　　電話：03-3944-6493（編集部）
　　　　　　　　電話：03-3944-6492（営業部・業務部）
　　　　　　　　http://www.kodansha-intl.co.jp

印刷 ──────── 日本写真印刷株式会社
製本 ──────── 牧製本印刷株式会社

落丁本・乱丁本は、小社業務部宛にお送りください。
送料小社負担にてお取り替えします。
この本についてのお問い合わせは、編集部宛にお願いいたします。
本書の無断複写(コピー)、転載は著作権法の例外を除き、禁じられています。

定価はカバーに表示してあります。

© HANAE MORI Co., Ltd., and Kodansha International Ltd. 2001
Printed in Japan
ISBN 4-7700-2684-6